Little Pebble™

Healthy Me

# I STAY ACTIVE

by Martha E. H. Rustad

CAPSTONE PRESS
a capstone imprint

Little Pebble is published by Capstone Press,
1710 Roe Crest Drive, North Mankato, Minnesota 56003
www.mycapstone.com

**Library of Congress Cataloging-in-Publication Data**
Names: Rustad, Martha E. H. (Martha Elizabeth Hillman), 1975- author.
Title: I stay active / by Martha E. H. Rustad.
Description: North Mankato, Minnesota : Capstone Press, [2017] | Series: Little pebble.
Healthy me | Audience: Age 4-7. | Audience: Grade K to grade 3. | Includes bibliographical
references and index. Identifiers: LCCN 2016032841
ISBN 9781515739821 (library binding)
ISBN 9781515739869 (paperback)
ISBN 9781515739982 (ebook pdf)
Subjects: LCSH: Physical fitness—Juvenile literature. | Exercise—Juvenile literature.
Classification: LCC RA781 .R796 2017 | DDC 613.7—dc23
LC record available at https://lccn.loc.gov/2016032841

**Editorial Credits**
Shelly Lyons, editor; Juliette Peters, designer;
Jo Miller, media researcher; Tori Abraham, production specialist

**Photo Credits**
Images by Capstone Studio: Karon Dubke
Photo styling: Sarah Schuette and Marcy Morin

Printed and bound in China.
007885

# Table of Contents

# Move!

I want to stay healthy!

I move for one hour each day.

My body stays active.

# School

I play at recess.

I hang from the monkey bars.

My muscles stay strong.

My class goes to P.E.

We play tag.

Running keeps
my heart healthy.

# Practice

I go to soccer practice.

We do a drill.

I stop a goal!

My sister tumbles.

I cheer for her.

She does a flip!

My brother swims.

He goes to a swim meet.

He swims fast.

# Outdoors

In winter we sled.

We climb up a steep hill.

I sled down.

Whee!

In summer we hike.

We find a path and walk.

We stop to drink water.

I play at the park.

I keep my body moving.

Staying active means

a healthy me!

# Glossary

**active**—being busy and moving around

**drill**—a kind of practice where you do a certain skill over and over

**heart**—a muscle that moves blood through your body

**hike**—to go for a long walk outside

**meet**—a sporting event with many races or contests

**muscle**—a band of body tissues that help the body move

**recess**—a break during school; students often play outside during recess

# Read More

**Coan, Sharon.** *Good for Me: Play and Exercise.* Time for Kids. Huntington Beach, Calif.: Teacher Created Materials, 2016.

**Meiners, Cheri J.** *Grow Strong!: A Book About Healthy Habits.* Being the Best Me!  Minneapolis: Free Spirit Publishing, 2016.

**Schuh, Mari.** *Get Moving!* What's On Myplate? North Mankato, Minn.: Capstone Press, 2013.

# Internet Sites

FactHound offers a safe, fun way to find Internet sites related to this book. All of the sites on FactHound have been researched by our staff.

Here's all you do:
Visit *www.facthound.com*
Type in this code: 9781515739821

Check out projects, games and lots more at
**www.capstonekids.com**

# Critical Thinking Using the Common Core

1. On page 18, what do they stop to do? (Key Ideas and Details)

2. Why is it important to keep your heart healthy? (Integration of Knowledge and Ideas)

3. What are muscles? Why are your muscles important? (Craft and Structure)

# Index